Cardboard Tube MANIA

Christine M. Irvin

Children's Press®

A Division of Scholastic Inc.

New York • Toronto • London • Auckland • Sydney

Mexico City • New Delhi • Hong Kong

Danbury, Connecticut

The author and publisher are not responsible for injuries or accidents that occur
during or from any craft projects. Craft projects should be conducted in the presence
of or with the help of an adult. Any instructions of the craft projects that require the use
of sharp or other unsafe items should be conducted by or with the help of an adult.

Design and Production by Function Thru Form Inc.
Illustrations by Mia Gomez, Function Thru Form Inc.
Photographs ©: School Tools/Joe Atlas

Library of Congress Cataloging-in-Publication Data

Irvin, Christine M.
     Cardboard tube mania / by Christine M. Irvin
       p. cm. — (Craft mania)
     ISBN 0-516-21674-0 (lib. bdg.)   0-516-27756-1 (pbk.)
     1. Paper work—Juvenile literature. 2. Paperboard—Juvenile literature.
     [1. Paperwork. 2. Paperboard. 3. Handicraft.] I. Title. II. Series.

     TT870 .I74 2001
     745.54—dc21

                                             00-0064386

CHILDREN'S PRESS and associated logos are trademarks and or registered trademarks of Grolier Publishing Co., Inc.
SCHOLASTIC and associated logos are trademarks and or registered trademarks of Scholastic Inc.

1 2 3 4 5 6 7 8 9 10 R 11 10 09 08 07 06 05 04 03 02

Table of Contents

Welcome to the World
of Craft Mania **4**

What You Will Need **6**

Crazy Kazoo **8**

Rain Stick **10**

Hair Holders **12**

Beautiful Bracelet **14**

Bunches of Bugs **16**

George the Giraffe **18**

Space Station **20**

Super Rocket **22**

Glowing Candle **24**

Toy Soldier **26**

Haunted House **28**

Daisy the Dog **30**

Index **32**

Welcome to the World of
CRAFT MANIA!

Don't throw away that cardboard tube! Everyday items, such as cardboard tubes and paper plates, can become exciting works of art. You can have fun doing the projects and help save the environment at the same time by recycling these household objects instead of just throwing them away.

You can find ways to reuse many things around your home in craft projects. Bottle caps, buttons, old dried beans, and seeds can become eyes, ears, or a nose for an animal. Instead of buying construction paper, you can use scraps of wrapping paper or even last Sunday's comics to cover your art projects. Save the twist ties from bags of bread or vegetables—they make great legs! These are just a few examples of how you can turn trash into art. Try to think of other things in your home that can be used in your crafts.

 # Did You Know?

- Each person creates about 4 pounds (1.8 kilograms) of garbage per day.

- Each person in the United States uses about 580 pounds (260 kg) of paper every year. Businesses in the United States use enough paper to circle the earth 20 times every day!

- Americans use enough cardboard each year to make a paper bale as big as a football field.

- Americans throw away more than 60 billion food and drink cans (like tin cans and soft drink cans) and 28 billion glass bottles and jars (like those from ketchup and pickles) every year.

That's a lot of trash!

What you will need

It's easy to get started on your craft projects. The crafts in this book require some materials you can find around your home, some basic art supplies, and your imagination.

Buttons, bottle caps, beads, old dried beans, or seeds for decoration

Glue

Tape

Tempera paints

Colored markers

Hole puncher

Construction paper (or newspaper or scraps of wrapping paper)

Felt (or scraps of fabric)

Twist ties (or pipe cleaners)

You might want to keep your craft materials in a box so that they will be ready any time you want to start a craft project. Now that you know what you need, look through the book and pick a project to try. Become a Craft Maniac!

A Note to Grown-Ups

Older children will be able to do most of the projects by themselves. Younger ones will need more adult supervision. All of them will enjoy making the items and playing with their finished creations. The directions for most of the crafts in this book require the use of scissors. Do not allow young children to use scissors without adult supervision.

☞ Helpful Hints

Cutting cardboard tubes can be tricky so make sure to get help from an adult. Pinching a part of the tube and making a small cut in a flattened section of tube makes it easier. Insert the scissors into the newly made slot and cut around the rest of the tube very carefully.

7

Crazy Kazoo

What you need

- One paper towel tube
- Hole puncher
- Pencil
- Ruler
- Waxed paper
- **Scissors** (Before cutting any material, please ask an adult for help.)
- Rubber band or hair elastic

What you do

1 Make an air hole in your kazoo. Using a hole puncher, punch a hole near one end of the tube, as shown.

2 Cover one end of your kazoo with waxed paper. Using a pencil and a ruler, measure and mark a 6-inch by 6-inch square on the waxed paper, as shown. Have an adult help you cut out the square.

3 Place the waxed paper on a flat surface, like a tabletop. Put the end of the tube, the one without the hole, in the center of waxed paper, as shown. Fold up the ends of the waxed paper around the tube, as shown. Hold the waxed paper in place with a rubber band.

Other Ideas

- Decorate your kazoo. Color it with markers or paint it with tempera paints before you cover the end with waxed paper.

- Experiment with kazoos, making several using different sizes of cardboard tubes.

Hair Holders

What you need

- One bath tissue tube
- Ruler
- Pencil
- Scissors (Before cutting any material, please ask an adult for help.)
- Tempera paints
- Paintbrush
- Hole puncher
- One craft stick

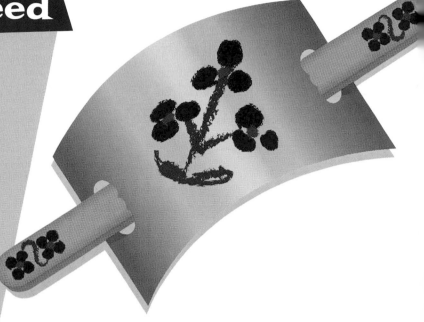

What you do

1. Cut out a hair holder. Mark a section of the cardboard tube, as shown. Make it as wide or as narrow as you like. Have an adult help you cut off the section along the marked line. To cut the tube, pinch about ½ inch of the tube between scissors and snip. Poke the scissors in the slot you've made and carefully cut around the tube, keeping the scissors as straight as you can. Then, have an adult help you cut the tube section in half lengthwise, as shown.

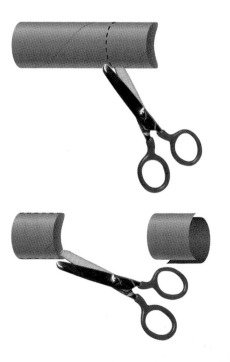

2 Use one of the half sections for each hair holder. Paint your hair holder with tempera paint, using any color you like. Let the paint dry before going on to Step 3.

3 Make two or three overlapping holes with a hole puncher, as shown. Slide the craft stick through the opening to hold it in place in your hair.

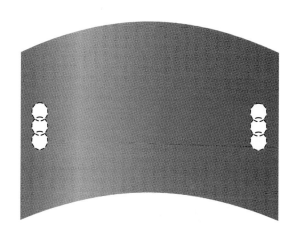

Other Ideas

• Add glitter to your hair holder.

• Cover your hair holder with fabric instead of painting it.

• Decorate the craft stick with different colored markers.

Beautiful Bracelet

What you need

- One extra wide wrapping paper tube
- Scissors (Before cutting any material, please ask an adult for help.)
- Tempera paints
- Paintbrush

What you do

1. Make a bracelet. Have an adult help you cut off a section of the wrapping paper tube, about 1 inch wide, or any size you want. To cut the tube, pinch about ½ inch of the tube between scissors and snip. Poke the scissors in the slot you've made and carefully cut around the tube, keeping the scissors as straight as you can.

14

2 Decorate your bracelet. Paint your bracelet with tempera paints. Let the paint dry before wearing your bracelet.

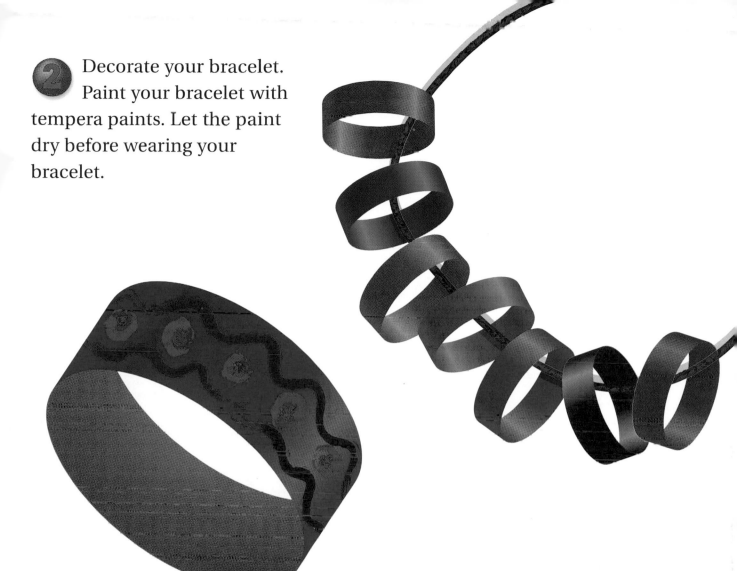

Other Ideas

- Make a necklace. Using a bath tissue tube, have an adult help you cut pieces of it about ½ inch wide for beads. Decorate the beads any way you wish. Then, string them on a piece of yarn or string to make a necklace.

- Add glitter, sequins, or buttons to your jewelry.

Bunches of Bugs

What you do

1. Make the bug's body. Have an adult help you cut off a section of the cardboard tube, as shown. To cut the tube, pinch about ½ inch of the tube between scissors and snip. Poke the scissors in the slot you've made and carefully cut around the tube, keeping the scissors as straight as you can.

16

2 Paint your bug's body any color you like with tempera paints. Let the paint dry before going on to Step 3.

3 Give your bug some legs. Twist ties from bags of bread or other food items make great legs. Put a drop of glue in the middle of each twist tie. Glue them to the middle of the bug's body, as shown. Let the glue dry before going on to Step 4.

4 Give your bug a face. Bend a twist tie to make an antennae and glue it to the bug's head, as shown. Using a marker, draw in a nose, mouth, and eyes. Let the glue dry before playing with your bug.

Other Ideas

- Use pebbles, buttons, or pieces of construction paper for eyes.

- Make a family of ladybugs. Paint the bugs with red tempera paint. Let the red paint dry. Then, paint some dots on your ladybugs using the black tempera paint. Let the paint dry before adding the legs.

George the Giraffe

What you do

1 Make the giraffe's body. Using a pencil, mark out the neck and legs on the cardboard tube, as shown. The neck should be about 5 inches long and the legs about 4 inches long. Be sure to mark out four legs. Have an adult help you cut along the marked lines.

18

2 Make the head and ears for your giraffe. Using the pencil, mark out the ears at the top of the tube, as shown. There should be only two marked lines, each about 1 inch long and about ¾ inch apart. Have an adult help you cut along the marked lines. Fold the cut piece back, toward the outside of the tube, to make the head, as shown.

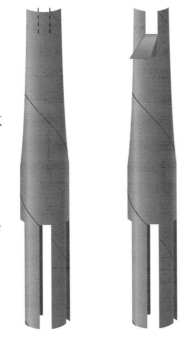

3 Decorate your giraffe. Paint the body with yellow tempera paint. Let the yellow paint dry. Add the patches by painting them on the body with brown tempera paint. Let the paint dry before going on to Step 4.

4 Finish your giraffe. Add eyes, hooves, and a nose with black paint. Let the paint dry before playing with your giraffe.

Other Ideas

- Make an assortment of giraffes using different-sized cardboard tubes. Set them up on your dresser or on a table for a neat wildlife display.

- Add pebbles, stones, or buttons instead of painting the eyes.

- Support the giraffe's legs with craft sticks for an extra sturdy animal.

Space Station

What you need

- Two paper towel tubes
- Two tissue boxes
- Tempera paints
- Paintbrush
- Large paper shopping bag
- Scissors (Before cutting any material, please ask an adult for help.)

- Glue
- One egg-holder section from an egg carton
- Markers or crayons

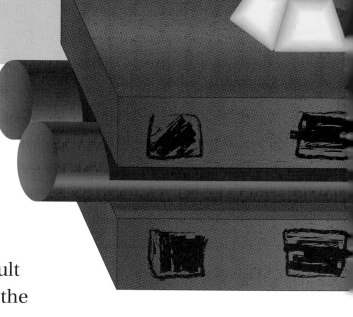

What you do

1 Paint the paper towel tubes with tempera paints. Set the painted tubes aside to dry.

2 Cover the tissue boxes. Have an adult help you cut a piece of paper from the shopping bag big enough to cover one tissue box. Spread a layer of glue around the tissue box. Wrap the paper around the box and press in place, as shown. Do the same thing with the other tissue box. Let the glue dry before going on to Step 3.

3 Glue the paper towel tubes together. Spread a layer of glue on one part of the paper towel tubes. Press the two paper towel tubes together. Set them aside to dry.

4 Glue the egg-holder section to a tissue box. Spread a layer of glue around the edge of one egg-holder section. Press it in place on top of one of the tissue boxes. Let the glue dry before going on to Step 5.

5 Put your space station together. Spread a layer of glue on the bottom of one of the tissue boxes. Press it in place on top of the paper towel tubes. Spread a layer of glue on the bottom of the other tissue box. Press it in place on the bottom side of the paper towel tubes. Let the glue dry before going on to Step 6.

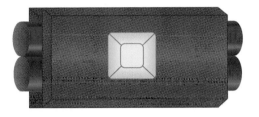

6 Add windows. Draw in windows using markers or crayons.

Other Ideas

- Make an international space station. Draw or paint flags from different countries on your space station.

- Make a space shuttle for your space station. Paint a small gelatin box with tempera paints. Glue two caps from toothpaste tubes to one edge of the gelatin box for engines. Draw in windows with markers or crayons.

Super Rocket

What you need

- **One paper towel tube**
- **Pencil**
- **Ruler**
- **Construction paper**
- **Scissors** (Before cutting any material, please ask an adult for help.)
- **Tape**
- **Glue**
- **One medium-sized piece of cardboard, such as the kind that comes with new shirts**

What you do

1 Cover your cardboard tube. Using the ruler and pencil, measure and mark an 11-inch by 4 ½-inch rectangle on the construction paper, as shown. Have an adult help you cut out the rectangle. Spread a thin layer of glue around the outside of the cardboard tube. Wrap the construction paper around the tube. Let the glue dry before going on to Step 2.

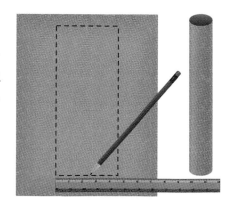

2 Make a cap for your rocket.
Find a cup or a mug (or a circle shape) that is about twice as big as the top of the cardboard tube. Place the circle shape on the construction paper and trace around it, as shown below. Have an adult help you cut out the circle. Then, have an adult help you cut the circle in half. Tape the cut edges of the circle together to make a cone shape, as shown.

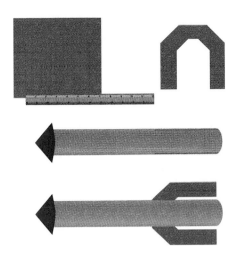

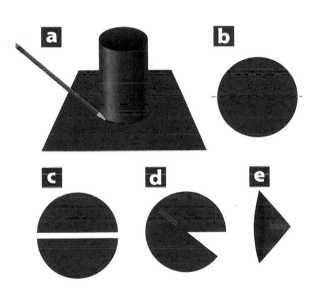

4 Add the rocket boosters.
Measure and mark the piece of cardboard, as shown above. The booster section should be about 6 inches high and 6 inches wide. Have an adult help you cut two slits in the sides of the rocket, as shown. The slits should be 6 inches long. Slide the booster section up through the slots, as shown.

3 Put the cap on your rocket.
Spread glue around the top of the tube and place the cone on top of it. The cone should hang over the edges of the tube. Let the glue dry before going on to Step 4.

Other Ideas

- Paint your rocket with tempera paints.
- Decorate your rocket with stickers or decals.

Glowing Candle

- One paper towel tube
- Pencil
- One thick paper plate or two thin paper plates
- Glue
- Tempera paints
- Paintbrush
- Orange and yellow construction paper
- Scissors (Before cutting any material, please ask an adult for help.)

What you do

1 Start your base. First, poke a hole with a pencil-point in the middle of the plate. If you are using two thin plates, poke a hole in the center of the second plate too. Next spread glue all over the inside of one plate. Place the second plate on top, lining up the holes, and press together. Set aside to dry well.

2 Make your candle. Paint the cardboard tube with tempera paint using any color you like. Let the paint dry before going on to Step 3.

3 Make flames for your candle. Using a pencil, draw flame shapes on the orange and yellow construction paper. Make one flame a little bigger than the other. Have an adult help you cut out the flames. Glue the two flame pieces together. Then, spread a thin layer of glue on the end of the flame piece. Glue the flame to the inside of the candle so that most of it sticks out at the top. Let the glue dry before going on to Step 4.

4 Make the hole in your base. Turn the plate upside down. Hold the candle in the center of the plate. Covering the hole in the middle of the plate, trace around the bottom of the candle. Poke your scissors through the hole you made earlier. Snip from the center out to the edge of the circle you traced. Make snips like that all around the circle. It will look like a flower.

5 Attach the candle to the base. Turn the plate upside down on a flat work surface. Spread a layer of glue around the bottom end of your cardboard tube (about 1 inch). Push the bottom of the cardboard tube through the hole until the bottom of the candle sticks out from under the plate about an ½ inch. Turn over the candle and plate. Press the petals of the flower to the glue on the candle. Stand it up and let it dry.

Other Ideas

- After you paint the cardboard tube, add a bit of glitter to the wet paint to make your candle sparkle.

- Cover your candle with construction paper instead of painting it.

- Decorate your candle according to the holiday or season. For instance, make red, white, and blue candles to celebrate Independence Day.

Toy Soldier

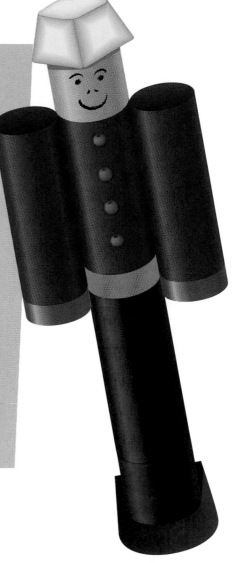

What you need

- One paper towel tube
- Two bath tissue tubes
- Pencil
- Ruler
- Tempera paints
- Paintbrush
- One egg holder section cut from an egg carton
- Small piece of lightweight cardboard
- Scissors (Before cutting any material, please ask an adult for help.)
- Glue
- Markers
- Small beads or seeds

What you do

1. Make the soldier's body. Measure down 2 inches from the top of the tube. Draw a line around the whole tube, as shown. This is where the soldier's body will start. Paint the tube, from the line down, with tempera paint. Let the paint dry. Measure down 4 inches from the top section. With the black marker, draw a thick line around the whole tube for the belt.

26

2 Add a face. Using markers, draw in the eyes, eyebrows, nose, and mouth in the top section the of tube.

3 Add the arms. Paint the two bath tissue tubes with tempera paint. Let the paint dry. Spread a thin layer of glue on one side of each tube. Press the tubes into place on the soldier's body, as shown. Let the glue dry.

4 Add a hat. Spread a thin layer of glue around the top of the soldier's head. Press the egg carton section into place on the soldier's head. Let the glue dry.

5 Add feet. Using the pencil, draw the feet shape on the piece of lightweight cardboard. Have an adult help you cut out the feet. Spread a thin layer of glue around the bottom of the soldier's body. Press the soldier's body in place on

the cardboard feet, as shown. Let the glue dry before going on to Step 6.

6 Add the details. Glue on small beads or seeds for buttons, or draw them in with a marker. Using the pencil, draw a thin line down the center of the soldier's body, from the bottom of the belt to the bottom of the tube, to indicate two legs. Do the same on the back of the soldier.

Other Ideas

- Turn your soldier into a tin man. Paint the paper towel tube and the tissue paper tubes with silver tempera paint before gluing the arms to the body. Use a paper cone for a hat.

- Turn your soldier into a robot. Paint the tubes and the bottle cap with silver tempera paint before gluing the arms to the body. Add nuts and washers for facial features.

HAUNTED HOUSE

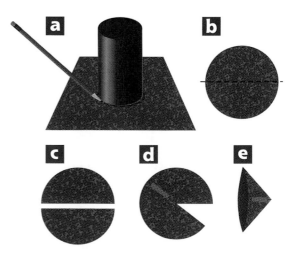

What you need

- Five or six cardboard tubes, each a different size
- Tempera paints
- Paintbrush
- Construction paper
- Pencil
- Scissors (Before cutting any material, please ask an adult for help.)
- Tape
- Glue
- One paper plate

What you do

1 Paint the cardboard tubes with tempera paints. Let the paint dry before going on to Step 2.

2 Make a roof for each tube. Find a cup or mug (or a circle shape) that is about twice as big as the tube. Place the circle shape on the construction paper and trace around it, as shown. Have an adult help you cut out the circle and cut the circle in half. Tape the edges of the half-circle together to make a cone shape, as shown.

28

3 Attach the roof to the tube. Spread glue around the top of the tube and put the cone on top of it. The roof should hang over the edges of the tube. Make one roof for each tube. Let the glue dry before going on to Step 4.

4 Put your haunted house together. Arrange your tubes to make a house shape, as shown. Experiment with the tubes until you have them arranged the way you want them. When you have decided how you want your house to look, glue the tubes to the paper plate. Let the glue dry before going on to Step 5.

5 Decorate the tubes. You can draw or paint windows and doors on your haunted house.

Other Ideas

- Cover your haunted house with construction paper instead of painting it with tempera paints.

- Give the outside walls of your haunted house some texture. Paint the tubes with tempera paints. Before the paint dries, dab a rough sponge around the outside of the tubes to make the paint bumpy.

- Add vines to the outside walls of your house by painting vines around the house with dark green tempera paint.

- Turn your haunted house into a castle. Paint the tubes with gray tempera paint (or cover with gray construction paper).

Daisy the Dog

What you need

- One paper towel tube
- One large brown grocery bag
- Ruler
- Marker
- Scissors (Before cutting any material, please ask an adult for help.)
- Glue
- Lightweight cardboard, such as the kind that comes with new shirts
- Pipe cleaner (for the tail)
- Felt (for the ears)
- Small buttons, seeds, or beads (for eyes, nose, and mouth)

What you do

1 Cover the cardboard tube with brown paper. Using a ruler and a marker, measure and mark an 11-inch by 5 ½-inch rectangle on the brown paper bag, as shown. Have an adult help you cut the paper. Then, spread a thin layer of glue around the paper towel tube. Wrap the paper around the tube. Let the glue dry.

2 Make the head and feet. Measure and mark the cardboard, as shown. The head needs to be about 6 inches high and 4 inches wide. The feet need to be about 4 inches high and 4 inches wide. Each leg should be about ¼ inch wide.

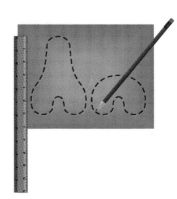

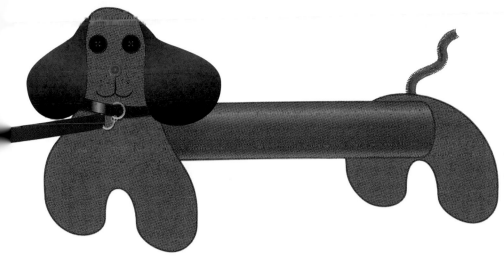

5 Glue the head to the body. Spread a thin layer of glue on one end of the cardboard tube body. Press the head into place and allow the glue dry before going on to Step 6.

3 Cover the head. Place the head piece on the paper, and trace around it. Trace the head piece again. Cut out the head shapes and glue the cutout paper to the front and back of the cardboard.

4 Cover the feet. Place the feet piece on the paper, and trace around it. Trace the feet piece again. Cut out the feet shapes. Glue one piece of the cutout paper on one side of the cardboard. On the other side, glue the pipe cleaner tail to the cardboard and then glue the cutout paper onto the card-board. Let the glue dry before going on to Step 5.

6 Glue the feet to the body. Spread a thin layer of glue on the remaining end of the body. Press the feet into place and allow the glue to dry.

7 Give your dog a face. Have an adult help you cut out two ear shapes from the felt fabric. Glue the ears into place on the head. Glue on buttons, seeds, or beads for the eyes, nose, and mouth.

Other Ideas

- Add a ribbon collar to your dog's neck.
- Paint your dog with tempera paints. Paint the cardboard tube and the head and feet pieces instead of covering them with brown paper. Let the paint dry before playing with your dog.

Index

Bracelet, 14–15
Bugs, 16–17

Candle, 24–25

Dog, 30–31

Giraffe, 18–19

Hair holders, 12–13
Haunted house, 28–29
Helpful hints, 7

Kazoo, 8–10

Rain stick, 10–11
Recycling, 4–5
Rocket, 22–23

Soldier, 26–27
Space station, 20–21
Supplies, 6

About the Author

Christine M. Irvin lives in the Columbus, Ohio area with her husband, her three children, and her dog. She enjoys writing, reading, doing arts and crafts, and shopping.